KARLA K. MORTON
NEW AND SELECTED POEMS

10

karla k. morton
new and selected poems

TCU press
FORT WORTH, TeXas

TCU Texas POETS Laureate series

Library of Congress Cataloging-in-Publication Data

morton, karla k.
  [Poems. Selections]
  New and selected poems / karla k. morton.
     p. cm. -- (TCU Texas Poet Laureate Series)
  ISBN 978-0-87565-414-0 (cloth : alk. paper)
  I. Title.
  PS3613.O77864A6 2010
  811'.6--dc22

                    2010004002

TCU Press
P. O. Box 298300
Fort Worth, Texas 76129
817.257.7822
http://www.prs.tcu.edu

To order books: 800.826.8911

Designed by fusion29
www.fusion29.com

This book is made possible by a generous Vision in Action grant from TCU.

THIS BOOK IS DEDICATED TO MY CHILDREN,
MATTHEW AND KATHRYN,
THE TWO GREAT JOYS OF MY LIFE.
MAY YOU NEVER GIVE UP ON THE POWER,
AND THE MAGIC, OF YOUR DREAMS.

table of contents

Introduction, Billy Bob Hill   1

Alamo Coastline   5

Searching for Ascension   6

For Love and Michelangelo   7

Becoming Superman   8

Charm Bracelet   9

Stone-Faced Men   10

Where Moonlight Cannot Tread   11

Bursting into Snowflakes   13

Electronic Quills   14

Superman's Birthday   15

Don't Be Nervous   16

Sailor's Delight   17

Pictographs   19

The *Real* Story of How Quanah Parker Brought the Wisdom of Jesus Christ to Native Americans   20

Still Wild   21

Wildfire DNA   22

Wild Pecans   24

What Clings to the Back of the Spoon   25

Tumbleweed Philosophy   26

Smoke Rings over Wichita County   27

Graveside in Sanger   29

Bad Theology   30

Christmas at Love Field   31

The Monarch and Her Mistress   32

(continues)

Confessions of a Laundromat Junkie 33

Shattering the Ordinary (a Superman shadorma) 35

Indian Blood 36

Inside Fat Quarters 37

Longhorned Angels 38

When Texas No Longer Fits in the Glove Box 39

Gypsy Envy 40

On the Podium 41

a.k.a. Elvis 42

Arachnid Platoon 43

Horse Latitudes 44

Clark and the Wolves 46

San Nicola Intercessions 47

Death and Soapboxes, Aisle 5 48

The Closer 50

Phobic 52

Hanging On 54

After 55

After the Floods in Gainesville 56

TOPLESS COCKTAILS DANCING NIGHTLY 57

Water 58

Meeting Tim 59

The Tightening. The Loosening 60

Memoirs of a Neighbour: The Moment Frost and I Became Friends 61

Clearing out the Irises 63

The New Hardscrabble 65

Dead Coyote Detour 66

(continues)

Why God Needs a Shotgun   67

If Only the Iceman Could Have Learned to Drive   68

Caliche Dust   70

Retirement: No Maydays   72

Living Close to DFW Airport, September 12, 2001   74

Stranded   75

Persistence   76

Fry Street Saints   78

Woman in the Pipe Shop   79

Coming of Age   80

Picking up the Accent   81

Acknowledgments   83

About the Author   85

introduction

The power of language has long fascinated karla morton. Her love of poetry began in grade school and continues in every book she writes. Currently, she is traveling on her Little Town, Texas Tour, as part of her appointment as Texas State Poet Laureate.

With this tour and in other efforts, karla morton is enthusiastically promoting, beyond her writings, poetry in general. Her participation in the enrichment of our state culture is in the tradition of such former poets laureate as James Hoggard, Larry Thomas, Alan Birkelbach, and the late Jack Myers.

The Fort Worth native, now of Denton, has had her work published in esteemed literary journals, electronic and in print. Morton's first-publication credits have appeared in such publications as *Amarillo Bay*, *REAL*, *descant*, *Langdon Review*, *New Texas*, *Illya's Honey*, *Borderlands*, and *Southwestern American Literature*.

Wee Cowrin' Timorous Beastie, her book/ CD released by Lagniappe in 2007, blends poetry and original music by the Canadian composer, Howard Baer. The poet followed *Wee Cowrin' Timorous Beastie* with *Redefining Beauty*, a book of poetry and photographs, published by Dos Gatos Press in 2009. In Redefining Beauty, morton writes from experience about her will to survive breast cancer.

This year will see this TCU Press collection in bookstores, along with three other new releases: *Becoming Superman* (Zone Press) *Stirring Goldfish* (Finishing Line Press) and *Names We've Never Known* (the Texas Review Press).

I didn't crunch the numbers from my manuscript copy of *karla k. morton: New and Selected Poems*, yet something like a third of content refers to a Texas time or place. The time is current day into recent past. Named communities include Gainesville, Sanger, Normangee, Robert Lee, Pampa, and Denton. Because I went to college in Denton, I particularly enjoyed "Fry Street Saints."

In some, Texas is like a character in a play, but in others, the setting serves a lesser purpose. A number of selections don't contain an exact regional reference.

Although "Bad Theology" does not divulge a given geography, it does portray a personality type that I've encountered more than once in Texas. No doubt, the type exists among the citizenry of the world. "Bad Theology" begins:

"She couldn't convince him

That he was a good man—

A kind man, a moral man...

He had grown up spoonfed

On brimstone and sinnery—

Told he was destined for eternal damnation.

       I appreciate the poetic technique in addition to the psychological study. Morton crafted "Bad Theology" without end rhymes. However, two interesting words, "spoonfed" and "sinnery," which finish off two lines, alliterate. In this way, the nicely placed alliteration lends form to the whole.

       Another poem that doesn't have a Texas place name, "Woman in the Pipe Shop," sends out sensuality as well as story.

"Amid the intoxicating scents

of man and leather,

and sweetened burley,

and latakia,

she kissed him—

a deep lover's inhalation."

       Below are the first stanzas of the fixed-form poem, "Persistence," which does take a sense of place from a specific Texas landscape.

"I follow the plains;

past the cotton; past the grain;

past the flat; past gold

hawks...And past

old

Amarillo, off a road—poured and

pocked, the plains dropped in a great

canyon! I gasped, stunned...

Two doves flew

out

of my eyes; doves, our birds, flew out of

my eyes; down; down, skimming rough,

palo duro rims...."

        Another poem, also with a Texas reference, is deserving of further recognition. An editor somewhere should anthologize "Living Close to DFW Airport, 2001." It's among the best poems about 9/11.

        "Living Close to DFW Airport, 2001" doesn't attempt the weight of September 11th. Rather using personal observation as metaphor, the poet recreates the day after.

"And how I cried, that September 12th,

standing in the driveway, face pressed

to the sky—listening, *searching*...

finding nothing but the drop-jaw shock

of Orion."

The reader again feels that collective numbness.

        These are only a few of the poems that give the reader delight. Diction, word play, and personal experience: there's much to find throughout this sixth collection in the Texas State Poet Laureate series from Texas Christian University Press. And inside this book, there is much to find in the gifts of karla k. morton.

Billy Bob Hill

Editor, The TCU Texas Poets Laureate Series

alamo coastline

There is no Statue of Liberty in Texas,
no huge lighthouse in the Hill Country
to guide wayward souls out of the dark
and home to safety.

But I met a man today, new to Texas,
and I asked him how he found his way here.
He stopped for a moment as his eyes filled...
and said back in '91,

he lost all three of his kids in a house fire.
Said he *had* to leave,
said he needed a place to go
to get away from their ghosts.

And he'd heard about Texas—
how the sky was so big,
how the sun burned pink before it set,
and thought...*maybe there*
he could find
enough space for his ghosts;
enough light
to lead him home through the dark.

searching for ascension

I feared I would never find you,
the windmill torn down—my trusty landmark.
Never stopped my truck to study it...never had to.
Windmills were built sturdy.
Water meant life.
Cattle have great faith.

I feared I would never find you,
progress and bettering tore down the windmill.
Had to learn to read road signs instead of horizons;
had to stop and stare at the hole in the dirt, in the sky.
The young take water for granted;
never think twice about thirsting cattle.

I feared I would never find you,
the steady, dependable life we knew, scattered
like rusting blades and long bolts in the turned up soil.
The asphalt under my tires, driving away the mice, the hawks;
bulldozers splitting time and earth and the flow of water, in two.
Not a cow to be seen.

I feared I would never find you,
but I turned my face into the wind, like Maine-Anjou—
muzzles moist and quivering; anxious for Earth's perfume;
trusting I would scent the Mecca of bovine dreams—
that ancient, spinning passion, coupling the broad shoulders of the wind
with the beauty of the clear, and rising waters.

For Love and Michelangelo

There is a memory in touch—
lips on a coffee cup,
feet in the sand,
bodies molded together in sleep,
your hand on my leg…

A hand so sure and strong…
it reminds me of standing in the Louvre years ago,
entranced by Michelangelo's slave sculptures.
I just couldn't resist running my hand
up one statue's calf to its thigh—
shuddering at the feel
of such amazing muscle definition in marble.

Guards, with machine guns,
immediately appeared,
not convinced when I explained
how sculpture was *meant* to be touched…
how it comes alive in the human hand.

It's a gesture so old and familiar…
One like the old master himself would have done—
a satisfied smile on his face…

A smile like yours now.
You stroke my skin
as though you've touched every inch of me
in another life;
back when chiseled marble was the photograph,
back when men took the time
to seduce beauty from a stone.

Becoming Superman

She thought it was all about the phone booth,
in fact, that's what impressed her most about him—
well, that and the flying thing;
and that one perfect curl…

But it was the *place* that changed him
which fascinated her—
that secret place you go
with your mundane baggage and worries;
that place that strips you down to your skivvies,
and you emerge,
confident,
hands on your hips,
flawless tights,
your cape, restless in the wind,
wearing the colour *you know* brings out your eyes,
stronger,
faster,
ready to leap…

CHARM BRACELET

I read about a woman who remembers *everything*.
It's a curse, she'd said, a disease
to *have* to remember every single moment of your life—
whether it be from 3 or 10 or 25 years ago.

How exhausting her life must seem,
to have the mundane as unforgettable as the remarkable—
the opposite extreme of Alzheimer's,
where all you have is this one moment, nothing before.

I've filled up two, almost three charm bracelets
with the many places I've been; with all my great adventures.
But lately, I find myself wanting
more silver charms—

wee historical markers
for all those moments I never want to forget;
moments I can recount to the grandchildren on my lap
as we finger through each silver glory of my life.

"Look, see this precious babe with wings,
to remember the day your mother was born.
And this one—an edelweiss flower,
to remember that Austrian village, where I first fell in love…

"Ah, and *this* one is my favourite—a tiny silver cup…
to remember how he curled his hand around the back of my neck,
and gently raised me up
to his lips…"

STONE-FACED MEN

Way up north, deep in the Canadian bush,
stand Inuksuit—
ancient stone men
built hundreds of years ago
by the Inuit Indians;
road markers to the villages,
or the rivers,
or the clearings;
reassuring comfort to all the weary souls
who traveled so long in the harsh wilderness.
You are not lost, they seem to say,
this is the way to go...

And in these modern times, it is these Inuksuit
who still mark the pathways the best—
when there's no electricity for lights;
when road signs would simply
rust in the elements.

Indeed, despite all the great scientific
advances in this world,
it seems in our most elemental of needs,
when we're lost and bewildered,
we still look to the power of man—
the wisdom of the old ways
in his head and his heart;
the steady strength of stone
in his arms.

where moonlight cannot tread

For as long as he could remember,
he'd wanted to be just like the moon.
round and white,
some traveler's compass in the dark,
one who inspired great love…
So he worked at it—
thinking moon thoughts,
sculpting himself into moon shape,
soaking in the sunshine each day
to practice glowing in the night.

Millennia after millennia,
he worked and worked
until one day, he did it—
he became the exact texture
and shape and size
of the orb he had seen
every night of his life.
But still, he was saddened,
knowing no matter
how hard or how long he tried,
he could never be
as bright or as brilliant…

It was then when she found him,
on top of that mountain.
She picked him up,
and put him in her pocket,
and took him home,
and cleaned him in her bath,
and set him on her nightstand,
on top of the Bible and Burns
and Birkelbach,
and Neruda's book of love poems.

(continues)

And that night
as she turned out her light,
and reached over
to feel his roundness once more,
he suddenly felt sorry for the big, cold moon...
For no matter how brilliant it was,
it would never know the dark pockets
next to a woman's round, warm hips;
or her sweet, secret sleep
inside the dark of drawn curtains.

Bursting into Snowflakes

"She died at play..." —Emily Dickinson

There wasn't a day that went by,
when she didn't look into the heavens,
and think of him—
her son, her bright, shining son.

He died on that soccer field
so long ago,
in full run;
a slight smile upon his nine-year-old face,

no trace of any pain;
as though his leap for the ball,
was a leap into the fall sky—
never feeling the ground he fell into;

his spirit breaking free
like a low, purple-dusted cloud—
suddenly...*silently*...
bursting into the soft, sweet storm
of a million wordless snowflakes.

—for Anne Baer, to honour the memory of her son, Scott

eLecTronic QUILLS

This is the pen of the modern-day lover...
though email's a tool for the entire world,
but just think of the others, so long ago—
who had to catch the bird,
to steal the feathers,
and pool the ink,
and press the papers,
before they could write even *one* word of love.

Oh, how they yearned with each slow curved letter,
to send their notes, flying through the air,
and pin them to the feathers of the gun-shy birds...
"I love you" were their words, *"Please hurry back."*
It could take weeks, months, even years.

The world has changed.
It has taken you and I
centuries to come together,
but now I tell you *"I give you my heart..."*
and it is yours, just 10 seconds later.

But the birds still remember
what was passed down through the ages;
they still remember the yearning
written on those pages.
See how they gather, out my window, undismayed—
each one of them singing
the song of your name.

superman's birthday

It wasn't that he was hard to please.
In fact, it was just the opposite—
he was so *easy* to be around…
and he appreciated *everything*.
But what do you give the man
who saves humanity on a daily basis?

But even Lex Luthor
didn't know his weakness
for the cream and the meringue…

So she baked him two pies,
and slipped into her favourite brown heels
and lead-free trench coat,
(after all, it was cold and rainy and January)
and took the pies up to his office—
watching him raise his right eyebrow
just slightly
over those dark-rimmed frames,
as he watched *her*
bend over
every man's desk,
and…ever so slowly…
serve each one of them
a warm slice of coconut cream.

DON'T BE nervous

when you see her.
Don't worry about
what you will say, or
how you will say it.
Just look at her,
and wonder
how your hand will fit
in the small of her back;
how many pins it takes
to hold up her hair…

sailor's delight

I wonder,
if I sit here long enough,
if I would become

part of this
reef; the dark mangroves curling
between my arms, toes;

mistaking
my bones for long bits of pale
coral; the lizards,

resting in
the shade of my thighs, their long
tails, curled up like brown,

thin, birthday
ribbon. Even the smallest
hermit crabs would make

their way up
to the rims of my ears, their
tiny, frail voices,

finally
audible—the larger male
complaining about

not enough
sex; the slightly smaller girl,
complaining that *he*

loves his job
more than her…I wonder if
the two of them had

(continues)

considered
moving in together. I
would want to ask them,

but my mouth
would be brimming in a small
lagoon, filled by high

tide, with two
tiny fish, darting side to
side, waiting for the

next big wave
to escape…That's what I would
do, if I were a

crab. I'd find
a larger, pre-owned shell we
both could fit into—

just enough
space for two desks, and a small
coffee pot. And we

would drive our
shell RV, with our many
Fred Flintstone crab feet

up to the
edge of the reef every night,
our scuttling legs

hanging out
over the delicate shell;
our four balloon eyes

watching the
island sky turn from yellow
to deep sailor's red.

PICTOGRaPHS

Were there no words,
I still would have loved you—
your eyes, soaking me in
like the rich drench of sunset
on canyon walls, and ledges
and ancient river bluffs.

Were there no words,
you would have dipped your wet fingertips
in the crushed red ochre—
slowly drawing *tenderness* behind my left knee;
desire, in the perfumed cleft of my neck;
ten arcs of *need* in the small of my back.

Were there no words,
I would have heard your love
in the turtle drum of your heart—
my head against your chest;
my painted body
illuminated in translation.

THE REAL STORY OF HOW QUANAH PARKER BROUGHT THE WISDOM OF JESUS CHRIST TO THE NATIVE AMERICANS

Just before you get to
the little Texas town of Quanah,
a road called 'Wisdom'
intersects Highway 287 North,
cutting due west through dirt
the colours of dark pink
and pink brown…
the same shades of a woman's
most tender anatomy.

I wonder if Quanah Parker himself
named that road…
recalling the way his lover, Weakeah, looked
the evening before,
when sunset
misted her naked body
in yet another layer of sheer glowing pinkness.
"Sweet God Almighty!"
Quanah must have muttered
in his native Comanche tongue.

A definite *come to Jesus* moment…

STILL WILD

A bit of her is still wild,
having been on her own for so long;
used to fending for herself;
used to finding her own shelter in the storms.

And every time I leave for a few days,
she becomes skittish again,
her self-preservation instincts kicking in—
claws and attitude defending her heart.

She doesn't want to love me;
doesn't want to *need* me—
need my hands on her neck; my words in her ear;
our nights curled together, the heat of our bodies giving, taking.

WILDFIRE DNa

There is something about fire
that leaves me in awe…
and despite its devastating destruction,
it holds such a primitive, mesmerizing beauty.

We humans are tricked, time and time again,
into thinking that fire has been tamed.
We take great satisfaction in striking a match—
in being able to hold something so powerful,
yet so tiny,
and wield it at will—
to the candle, to the fireplace, to the stove…

But still, after living side by side with humans
for thousands of years,
one wildfire tells us
there is no domestication.

Not even in the single flame that sits gentle on the table,
seemingly as innocent as the cat upon my lap,
small and sweet and purring…
yet she can turn on you,
in the middle of that ear-rub,
instantly drawing blood;
turning from Tigger to Tigress
in a matter of seconds, for no other apparent reason
than the time was right;
knowing she shares her DNA with that great wild beast
who answers to no man…

(continues)

Indeed, this cold winter's night seems picturesque;
seems domesticated enough—
the gentle, sleeping cat,
the warm and lovely fireplace...
Yet they sit, calm and curled and waiting;
waiting with the patience of time;
waiting for that perfect combination
of hunger and air and proximity
to turn on you—
unleashing all that is
primitive and feral and murderous
from their ancient and devouring souls.

WILD PECANS

wooden flowers fall
golden manna for lovers
one pecan, two tongues

WHAT CLINGS TO THE BACK OF THE SPOON

There was no mention
of spareribs
or chicken-fried steak
and gravy…
but then, *that* was a lesson
we could have easily taught *them.*

But when I asked
about *their* favourite food,
they spoke of
growing up in England
with Mum's onion soup,
and Scotch eggs,
and cheese and pickle sandwiches.
Their eyes clouded,
and they had to clear their throats
to get back to the day's lesson
about foie gras and mirepoix,
and how you know the crème is *perfect:*
when it clings
to the stirring spoon.

And I realized then,
how much alike we all were
in that little French Cookery,
a spoon in every hand,
because what it all boils down to,
no matter where you're from,
is the way Mum smiled and said your name,
as she called you in
to set the table for supper.

TUMBLEWEED PHILOSOPHY

I could never resist the trains,
all that power and steel and energy.
I still stop and wave and count the cars
as they rumble by.

And on a road trip along 287,
we came upon a train
racing along the highway, side by side
with summer's blurred cornfields.
And I unbuckled as we neared the main engine,
took off my glasses,
and leaned heavily out the passenger window,
hair loosed and wild in that 75 mile per hour whip,
frantically waving both arms
until the conductor sounded the horns,
and I blew him a theater kiss...

Smiling, I buckled back into my seat;
back into the boundaries
of appalled teenagers
and a chastising husband.
My hair, teased and swollen,
full of feed lot air
and bits of raw cotton
from the flatbed in front of us
on its way to the gin.

I waited a long time
before I even attempted
to detangle my ball of tussled hair,
revelling in the freedom
of being manhandled by the wind...
wondering if *this* was how
the tumbleweeds felt,
as they rolled and laughed
and jumped the Panhandle plains;
before they got caught in the barbs
of the taut and rusting wire fences.

smoke rings over wichita county

We went to Wichita Falls every few months
to see the girls.
It was *always* about the girls:
Minnie, Lurline, Roberta, Oleta,
Genevieve, Novella, Adell…
And when they all got together,
and began to eat and drink
and gossip and laugh,
they'd kick up a cloud of female
so thick, it seemed to choke the men,
who all *suddenly* needed a cigarette
at the exact same time.

It was good. All so good
and familiar and happy.

Our trips there became less frequent
with time and sickness and death…
until, ultimately, the last sister
was gently laid down in her Sunday best
and favourite earrings…
and the only laughter left
came from the wind chimes in the old elm tree
which now covered them all.

We went up again later, with the kids,
wandering among the family
in a slow, red-granite hopscotch,
still unsettled by the fact
that they were all gone;
that all their happy gatherings had ended.

And returning on Highway 287, I kept looking back,
trying to remember what scrying included
rear-view mirrors and pot-holes, and the big Texas sky…
Whatever would the future bring?

(continues)

This old road was so familiar,
but one we wouldn't travel for a long, long while.

And I looked back again in the mirror,
feeling torn and empty, when *suddenly*,
there, in the open blue, a big group of clouds
had gathered above the fading Wichita skyline—
all standing in a circle; all leaning into each other
like old men stepping out for a smoke.

Graveside in Sanger

It was what funeral weather should be—
pale, winter-dead grass,
the mean bite of February
clamping down through your coat,

through your Sunday pants;
pain inside and out
letting you know
you are still alive.

And the men…all those big, Texas men,
standing too stiff—
wishing they were anywhere else in the world
in that moment;

all staring down
during the deluge of *Amazing Grace*;
hands hard-fisted behind their backs;
nails digging into their palms;

men who hadn't cried since childhood;
men who had learned, from their fathers,
how to force their tears down,
through the soles of their restless boots.

Bad Theology

She couldn't convince him
that he was a good man—
a kind man, a *moral* man.

He had grown up spoon-fed
on brimstone and sinnery—
told he was destined for eternal damnation.

So ironic, she thought,
that religion made God's work so much harder;
kept so many good people *away* from the church.

But she hoped God worked His magic out there,
when he was out on the plains—
the morning mist rising off the river;

his long, strong legs
wrapped tight around the warm muscle of the horse,
his breath, rounding in perfect halo about his head.

CHRISTMAS AT LOVE FIELD

They called it the swarming season—
that mild Texas winter in late December,
when the birds gather
like big black nets in the sky

—hundreds of them—
simultaneously hovering and circling;
then suddenly swooping down to the earth,
then repositioning, then rising back up,

and around; then landing once more
over and over again,
until instinct kicked in
and they collectively swelled up together,

and flew away,
each going to the sanctuary of their own nests...
And inside the airport,
swarms of people came and gathered,

and sat and swelled and rushed—
all beckoned by the pull of the season;
by that ancient, instinctual homing-call
of Christmas.

THE MONARCH AND HER MISTRESS

There was something about her
that stoked the soul;
a rekindling that made the heart beat
a little faster,
the lungs breath
a little deeper.

Long limbed and elegant,
old enough to have
walked in beauty,
as well as owned it;
possessing an aura that drew others in
like the irresistible scent of gardenias;
like cool fat grass to the toes.

In God's great plan,
we were made for each other—
the trees, feeding oxygen;
humans, carbon dioxide…
Even the Native Americans call them
the Standing People—
our extended family on this good earth walk.

But it's hard for me to separate The Monarch—
that grand, old live oak in the Inge's garden—
from her Mistress.
Indeed, rarely can I think of one, without the other.
Both possess a stillness—a grace
born unto them,
yet nurtured and fed
through the many years
by the constant poetic exhalations
of all those Texas Laureates
who have clustered around
their genteel feet.

—for Dominique Inge

In September 2010, the Monarch will be renamed the Texas Poets Laureate Tree. The
dedication will commemorate the many Poets Laureate of the State of Texas who have
read their poetry beneath the boughs of this great live oak. The tree lives on the property
of Charles and Dominique Inge in Granbury, Texas.

confessions of a laundromat junkie

I love the way it smells in here.
The clean, the soaps,
the hint of warm metal.
All that cleanliness and godliness
for about 20 quarters.
I just can't get enough of it.
All that dirt coming in
only to be washed in absolution
and sent back out unto the world again
pure and chaste for another week.

Dirty laundry pours into
those little round windows.
"Forgive me, Father, for I have sinned."
Sloth potato chip stains
cover my pants,
marinara gluttony
crosses my shirt,
lipstick lust
marks my collar.

Penance must be paid,
so I gather all those stray pennies
that snuck into the wash,
now shiny and clean,
and hide them, *heads up*
in the missing tile pieces
of that old laundromat floor...
a little game I play
with some unknown child—
manna from heaven
on a boring Monday night.

(continues)

And I always leave
feeling a little better, a little lighter,
and, acting on the overwhelming urge
to love thy neighbour, I
DWJWD
(do what Jesus would do),
and tithe my last two quarters
to the red-headed cutie
in the blue Texas Rangers cap.

SHATTERING THE ORDINARY
(a superman shadorma)

He tried them,
again and again:
timepieces.
But he kept
crushing them on rogue airplanes
and meteorites.

Once, even,
a thankful city
presented
him a watch…
That one was a gold Rolex—
(it was his favourite)…

He forgot
he was wearing it
when the train
had derailed—
it had no chance between steels.
"Damn," was all he said.

But Lois
didn't mind at all.
She rather
liked the man
who donned the ordinary
and then shattered it…

INDIAN BLOOD

Great grandma insisted
there was Indian in our blood.
Having crossed from California

to Texas in a covered wagon,
it broke down in Arlington, where
her father built the big house,

which she promptly fell from, head
slamming hard against a milk pail
two stories down. Years later,

completely blind, she swore she'd
heard the scandal whispered right
there in the house, ears keen beyond

the sighted. Embarrassed, the family
scoffed, offered up four blue-eyed,
tow-headed great-grandchildren

as proof: Simply impossible. One
day, she asked me to describe the
sunset, upset that she'd forgotten pink.

I said it was the smell of face cream;
her newborn babies; the roses
climbing the back fence. She

smiled, pulled me close, and asked
if I ever heard flutes in the rush of the river,
if the wind ever called me by name.

Inside Fat Quarters

Finishing up the stitches, knotting my initials and
the year into the corner of this quilt…I'm done.
Two years it took for this one—moving quickly at
first, then waiting for every 15 minutes of strength

and free time to sew another block. It held me,
stitch by stitch, through fear and chemotherapy,
my bare head buried in its ambers and browns,
tears flowing once, right there, on the sewing table;

each stitch, pulling me through, back into the light;
back into faith, with the promise of nights under
the moon on cool grasses; of mountain vacations
in front of a fire—that sacred transformation of wood

to scent, permeating each fiber; of Friday night
football games, between bleachers and blue northers—
spills of hot chocolate staining its pinwheels and
panels and unmatched points. Mother taught me,

years ago, that perfection didn't matter—it's all about
strong seams and three layers, whatever they may be…
some Depression quilts having only newspapers
between them…I loved the idea, tucking bits of old

blankets inside the kids' new ones, layering years and
stories upon them each night. Even the dog seemed to
understand the quilt's magic, curling up on this one as
soon as I stretched it out for a finished look. But first,

it will hold you and I down at the river bottom,
spreading a picnic; then after, we'll wrap up together,
heads sticking out like natives in an R. C. Gorman print.
And I'll tell you down there, where tree roots drink the creek,

that if you had a native name, it would be *One Who
Makes the Woman Sing;* and you'll smile, and kiss
away all words, and lay me down inside those fat
quarters; and make your name come to life.

LONGHORNED ANGELS

To tell the truth, she felt left
out. All the descendents named
Blanche, decreed to
spend one night at the Edgecombe Manor in

Alabama, in Great-Aunt
Blanche's room...where she'd come back
from the dead, to
stand in the window, to have a look at

them. "But you're just not a Blanche,"
her mother would simply say...
But one night at
an old, fenceless ranch house west of Georgetown,

she woke to a huge longhorn
staring in the window, his
great round nostrils
steaming patches on the cool glass...*This land,*

she thought, was where she belonged—
where no ghost dare cross the paths
of night rattlers;
where longhorned angels keep watch until dawn.

—for Margaret Edge Chalfant

WHEN TEXAS NO LONGER FITS
IN THE GLOVE BOX

Once you unfold a road map of Texas, your world is changed.
Towns like Falfurrias, Carthage, and Maypearl suddenly become
part of your life...and, once you see them, you can't go back to
not knowing them. You *have* to go there—even if it's just
with your eyes—or your finger—tracing those
crow's feet county roads into unexplored territory.
That's how knowledge works. *That's* how knowing works.
Life is expanded; there's *no* going back.
There's no refolding the map.

It's like meeting an alarmingly charming man...
discovering his dangerous detours and thrilling new paths,
finding unforeseen forks and magnificent natural beauty.
You'll look up at him and know that the crinkly arch between his eyes
goes from Childress up to Amarillo, then back down to Muleshoe;
that the whites of his nails reach from Huntsville to Jasper;
that his green eyes encompass the metroplex—
from Fort Worth to Denton to Dallas.

And you can't help but imagine that the crooked hairline
beneath his navel would run all the way down Highway 281,
and across the border, into dark, exotic Mexico;
or that his lips could take you on incredible road-trips—
stretching clear across the state—from El Paso to Nacogdoches
with just a smile;
or that the best kiss of your life
would whisk you through the wild-flowered Hill Country,
and leave you weak-kneed and breathless
along the Riverwalk in old San Antone...

GYPSY envy

I have a friend who says he's happiest when he's moving—
between states, between cities, it didn't matter.
It feels so good, he says, to have everything you own
boxed up and packed tight in the trailer behind you—
knowing at each stoplight, or at each highway exit,
you could just turn left...or turn right...

And I thought how similar that is to the life of a poet—
always reaching; always searching for answers;
always traveling down new thought pathways
with everything we've ever accumulated—
everything we've ever seen and tasted
and touched and read and smelled,
flung together in the carpet-baggage of our brain.

I guess we're both just gypsies at heart...

But then we see those tiny songbirds, racing by, premeditated;
quickly zooming in, tucking into the tiny, innermost, branches of a
tree,
always able to alight perfectly, effortlessly,
so sure of their path;
so sure of their *exact* destination.
Their thoughts,
never plagued by uncertainties;
never *once* burdened
by rolled rugs and cardboard boxes,
and the scattered, empty circles of packing tape...

on the podium

I could imagine God like that—
tall, strong shoulders
enhanced in black tuxedo tails;
passion blossoming his face;
desire pulsing through his body
as he called forth, from the silence,
the music of the stars and the moon
and the rising sun;
the pull and push of his arms
birthing the mountains and the beasts
and the tiny blooming flowers;
the hush of clouds forming
as one finger pressed to his lips.
A masterpiece brought to life;
the symphony of earth
mixed with the complex harmonies of the human soul—
of power and sex and divinity;
both hands thrown up to the heavens
in magnificent creation!

But the rains
came on their own
as the sky swelled, spellbound;
listening...
watching from behind;
weeping at the beauty
of it all.

—ekphrastic poem inspired from Barber's *Adagio for Strings*
conducted by Dr. Scott McCormick, Langley Virginia
20 Apr 08

a.k.a. elvis

Back in the fifties, he went a little wild.
For years he'd been tormented with cries from every land:
Rescue *our* soldiers! *Our* cause is true!

Sure, there were villains, but how do you save a people you love
from the hate of one another?
The war was *finally* over. The world seemed a bit more peaceful...

So he let his curl and sideburns go, and perfected his hip-swivel,
and took to the stage, knowing full well that the heat from the lights
and his black leather pants (over blue tights) would build up a sweat,

releasing super-pheromones,
which would whip every female within 200 miles into a hormonal
frenzy.
The population soared! They called him *The King!*

And for a while, the world danced...
But years passed; people got restless—got ugly again.
Knowledge became the price for immortality.

The record company had to hire a body double
because he was so distracted—
helplessly watching earthlings kill each other;

secretly wishing for a planet-threatening asteroid
to bind them all together in one great cause.
But as much as he wished for peace, Superman knew better—

he knew that no amount of unconditional love,
or miracles of strength,
or hound-dog rock and roll,
could *ever* save a world that just didn't want to be saved.

arachnid platoon

They come every night, descending with the dusk;
silent paratroopers, dropping down, just barely into view.

Heroes, locked and loaded, spinning their masterpiece
in air and twig camouflage,
ready to snare all those kamikazes
coming after me and the yellow porch light.

And after their work is done, we sit together
with our cocktails—wine of the grape and of the moth,
watching those same moths
drink the sweet white nectar of the moonflowers;

listening to the songs of the tree frogs,
and the padded footsteps of the possums
racing across the wooden fence tops.
But the spiders never say a word, even when I ask

what happens to their web every morning;
wondering if it gets knocked down by all those moths
in their celestial navigation towards the light;
or if *they* take it down, methodically, rope by rope,

like a soldier wrapping up his parachute;
his country's secrets tucked safely in the dark.

Horse Latitudes

It was the Spaniards who introduced
the first horses to America—
those amazing, magnificent creatures
that completely changed the culture of our country.

They brought them over to this New World
in their great three-masted galleons—
hundreds at a time—
and though many made it through,
there was a place along that journey,
toward the West Indies,
that both man and beast began to fear...

It was close to the Equator, where the winds
would suddenly stop—
for hours, for days, for weeks;
those huge ships simply sat on the water;
their tall, white sails
limp in the unyielding air.

The Doldrums, they were called,
but these were worse.
They were hotter and drier, and lasted so long
that the food and water supplies
ran dangerously thin—
forcing the men
to throw their prized Mustangs overboard;
and watch their floating corpses
hover in the unmoving currents,
until the sharks arrived...

(continues)

And as we sail through those ancient waters,
I look deep into the gentle sea,
well-fed by such tragedies;
and say a prayer for all those trusting steeds,
and for their Conquistadors,
who, with tears in their eyes,
had to lead their beloved Rosinante,
or Baiardo, or Incitatus, or Marengo,
to the edge of the ship,
and make sure their swords
were mercifully sharp…

And I looked up into the sky,
to the all-seeing heavens,
and whispered one more prayer
for the stars—
thinking how haunted they must be
to have witnessed such visions;
understanding why they never
seem to sleep.

clark and the wolves

He used to play with them,
growing up on the old Kent homestead—
the pack mistaking
the lean, muscled reach of his forearms,
and the chiseled angles of his face
as one of their own.

san nicola intercessions

The Captain insisted he was a modern man—
not weakened by all the superstitions
of his fellow Italians down in Bari.

Sure, he had grown up
learning, and reading, and wishing on
the saints and the stars of the sailors,
but this was the *new* world
of mathematics, and computers, and high-tech electronics,
and he was a schooled man—
too skeptical and too educated
to still believe in such old-world magic...

But when we came upon that little capsized boat
Christmas morning—
500 miles too far west
between Cuba and Florida,
he ordered search and rescue maneuvers,
and dispatched his crew,
and alerted the Coast Guard...

then crossed himself,
his hands,
unconsciously deploying saintly aide
to the lost seamen;
his heart,
still hoping for a Christmas miracle...

death and soapboxes, aisle 5

There was this photographer
who came to the States to open a studio.
It surprised him, though,
that Americans didn't photograph their funerals,
and he pulled out a picture
to show me what he meant:

It was an old Asian man,
dressed in black,
sitting hunched over—
his hands, cupping his grieving face.

Now, with a photographer's eye,
I could see the raw beauty of it
in the unadorned walls,
the simple stool,
the pure emotion of the moment.
But I had to turn away.
It was too *much,* too painful.

He didn't understand my reaction.
"It is *life,*" he said.
"It is *death,*" I said.
"But it's no different than the movies,
or the newspapers, or songs...
or your poetry," he added.

He was right, of course.
So what was so unsettling
about an 8 x 10 glossy?

(continues)

Maybe I need to be able
to *choose* when I see such pain,
to choose to read a book,
to choose to see a two-hanky movie,
to choose to drive to the cemetery.
I don't want grief ripping me open
like a sliver of broken glass
each time I pass the hallway,
and walk into the kitchen for a cup of tea.

I wonder if he's traveled around here,
that foreign photographer.
He would enjoy shooting all those
little white crosses along the roads,
marking the places people have died…
all that death posing
in plastic-flowered Kodak moments.

Imagine if everyone did that—
every median would be filled,
hospitals would have no room to operate,
even the grocery stores
would have to build extra shelves
to accommodate all those hearts
that just gave out on aisle 5,
in between the canned carrots
and the cut green beans.

THE CLOSER

They talked about it often—
about the best way to die, and the worst.

They had seen it all, knew all the signs—
declining urine output, bluing nails,
rising temperature, chain-stoking breath...

But some patients would hang on, despite these sure signs—
long passed the time when their body
should have simply given up;
long past their family's emotional and physical limits.
And that's when they brought her in—
the one they called *The Closer*.

She would fly into the room, clad in bright clothes;
cursing the road, and the traffic; hinting of a fresh cigarettes;
and lift that dark, dank room, full of weeping and doom,
with a wicked smile, and an off-coloured joke,
introducing herself irreverently to everyone there—
saying who she was; what time it was;
saying she was there to send everyone of them off—
bon voyage, farewell, arrivaderci, vaya con Dios.

And she would tell the family to say their good-byes,
and go out together, somewhere, to eat, or drink, or smoke, or just drive...
because *some people just don't want to die with everyone watching.*

And sure enough they would—every time...
the family would leave, and the dying would die.

So many people asked what the secret was
to her Hospice badge of honour,
but she'd just shrug her shoulders, and joke in her hard, gruff voice,
I guess I can just close the deal.

(continues)

But the day she came for *us*, and told *us* to go,
I lingered, hiding behind the door,
and watched her open the window,
though it was dark and freezing outside…
And she sat by my mother, and gently took her hand,
and whispered something inaudible,
but in a tone so low and heartfelt,
it brought tears to my eyes.

And I felt the sudden swirl of soft breeze;
smelled the perfume I remembered from so long ago;
and turned my eyes to the opening of the window—
knowing Death had come and swept the room;
knowing her soul had become
the same colour as the wind.

PHOBIC

(for Sandy)

I have a friend I love dearly,
who tends to be very…phobic,
who sells medical supplies,

and who, unfortunately, is very
aware of every disease known
to man. He doesn't do public

toilets or water fountains. He
washes his hands exactly 32 times
every day. He counts every stair;

every repeating pattern.
He likes to come to my house
on Fridays, knowing it's just been

cleaned; knowing no one
has used the guest bathroom.
He accepts my clutter, my

inability to throw things away;
just as I accept his need for
paper towels at every sink;

his desire for only crunchy foods.
He came over, after moving
into his new house…and I listened

(continues)

to him vent; understanding how he
disinfected the seat in his new
shower seven times, but how he

still can't use it, knowing some
88-year-old woman's naked butt
once called it her own.

HANGING on

When the Alzheimer's set in
she clung to her coat hangers.

Not the big plastic ones, or the padded girly ones,
but those old, bendable wire ones she had used
every day of her life,
in every load of laundry, in every closet,
on every campout.

She would hug them to her breast
with both arms, terrified to let go.

At night, she would hide the extras
under the mattress
or in the drawers
so no one would steal them.

And in the mornings,
she would put on as many clothes
as she could, layer after layer,
so she could keep the empty hangers in her hands.

The curve of the hook,
the twist in the neck,
the thin triangular labyrinth
held her busy fingers and idle memory
when *our* faces, *our* names could not.

It was the one thing she could remember about her life.
The one thing she could hang on to
that still held purpose,
that could somehow lead her back
to clarity...
if she could
just
hold
them
tight enough.

after

It's after.
It's after the pain, the shock,
the trip to the ER.
After the look in the doctor's eyes,
and the tears,
and screaming into your pillow.
After the house swells
with friends and family and neighbours.
After everyone has come,
and cried, and touched, and eaten,
and gone.
It's after church.
After the words have been said,
and the songs have been sung,
and the earth has been put back together.

After the glossy-eyed mourners
have traveled back home.
After.
After thank-you notes have been written.
After the excess food has been discarded,
the ringing phone settled,
and the house is quiet again.

It's *then*.
Then, when you're sitting alone on the sofa doing laundry,
folding the warm, white t-shirts
that still hold his smell...

It's *then* when death gently
taps upon your shoulder
and whispers:
"I have come."

after the floods in gainesville

I walked the Square

Laced in the open-air with blooming crepe myrtles --
Opulent heads, hanging low
Vandykes of pinks saturated with weeks of rain.
Enchanted, I had to know…I cupped one in my

Hands and water flooded and ran through my fingers…so
I raised another to my lips, and drank in the sips of cool rain,
Sweetened with the stain of fuchsia flowers.

He smiled as I turned, and cupped *my* cheeks
As they burned in his palms; pulled me close…closer.
Niched there, under the eaves of the dripping wet leaves,
Deliciously feasting on another hot pink deep drink of
Summer magic.

TOPLESS

COCKTAILS

DANCING NIGHTLY

It was my dad's favourite story—
how he and his soldier buddies
were tricked into a bar one night
with the sign:

TOPLESS
SERVERS

(they were, of course, all men).

I laughed every time he told it...
My kids, however, never saw the humour—
rolling their eyes even now
as we pass this *new* billboard,

when I remark how lucky the martinis have it
at the end of the night—
their tossed off Vandyke sweaters
so easily spotted in all the tiny piles of laundry
pooling in the rings
of empty wine glasses
and naked highballs...

water

Up in the Panhandle, it's all about the water.
Cattle gather at the prairie windmills
in hopes of a strong wind, for a good deep drink,

Shade is a luxury out there—
and the few trees that grow
have been planted by human hands

at rest-stops, or around houses—
nourished by bathwater and rain barrels
and yesterday's leftover iced-tea.

And when winter comes, they even grow thankful
for the bitter snow and ice,
which pierces the scrub and the sage—

knowing it will make its way
through each thawing level of dry earth,
back over to the stilled windmills;

the thirsty cattle, bellowing, *beckoning* the wind;
their short, furry ears, poised and waiting
for that first tiny squeal of metal against spinning metal.

MEETING TIM

He talked about his time there, in Guam;
about how clear the water was; about
night diving 150 feet—so deep, yet
you could look up through the water,

and see the closest stars, and the
silhouettes of passing sharks. He
said it was an odd kind of safe
down there—away from war;

where tiny fish would gather around him,
as though he were some deep sea god
in a halo of minnows as thin and iridescent
as the fleeting new moon.

THE TIGHTENING. THE LOOSENING

His mind tended to wander when he drove out,
checking the fence lines;
wondering if his great-granddad would've had something to say
about the luxury of a truck, when all that perfectly good horseflesh
waited back in the stalls, needing to be exercised anyway.
Two birds, one stone... he'd say.
But the truck was so efficient. Some battles never change—
time and rain and rattlers.

He could have sent one of the hands out to check the fences,
but it was one of the few pleasures he gave himself—
looking out over his beloved land, knowing it still looked the same
as it did hundreds of years ago, way before his great-grandfather's time.
He kicked aside a curling snakeskin, eyeing the shadows
around the fencepost.
He wondered if it felt good to a snake to shed its skin;
decided it did.

Something there is that doesn't love a fence... he thought, getting out again
to upright a post; tighten the wires. He wondered what that Frost fellow would've
had to say about West Texas—the wild of horses; the constant drought;
rattler ghosts at every step...
He wondered about the future—about too many people chewing up the land;
crowding the earth. Used to, you had to birth a lot of kids to help with the ranch,
but these were the days of fast trucks and hungry Mexicans—
their mothers, destitute across the border.
And as he pulled off his gloves, he found himself thankful
to be living in this modern age—glimpsing his great-granddad's knuckles,
strong and sun-scarred—that same DNA snaking around inside of him...
And he wondered about the past—if *his* hands
could have ever cracked a whip against a dark man's back,
even if he thought it was the only way
to save the land he loved.

memoirs of a neighbour:
the moment frost and i became friends

It was late one night,
and the Derry air
held the raw musk
of earth and frost and bovine.

1899 had been a long year—
with turn of the century fears
of a lost age, and the unknown future…
But it was also a change mixed
with a ripe sensation;
a Christmas current;
a stirring in all of creation for,
shall we dare say…
hope?

And as I walked along the moonlit path,
my ears felt especially keen
to the crunch of the snow at my feet;
to the rhythm of my breath;
to the stillness of that Christmas Eve.

A myth had long prevailed in my heart:
that animals spoke in human tongue
during that short, magical moment of midnight,
when the miracle of Christmas was upon us—
a childhood fantasy I stoked every year;
a hope that called me out
to this very untraveled, rural path.

I pulled out my timepiece,
straight up midnight. Oh! *Christmas!*

It was *then* when I heard it,
the odd rustle of cow bell and muffled voice.
I held my breath and quickly tucked behind
the fatted tree in the path,
careful not to disturb the miracle unfolding.

(continues)

It wasn't so much a cry…but a cadence,
a rhythm…*sweet God!* A cow with human tongue!

      Vox Clamantis in Deserto
      Vox Clamantis in Deserto

Och! How perfect!
A dairy cow in the most holiest of hours,
in a field in New Hampshire…
speaking Latin!

I walked up closer…and the voice stopped.
A figure *leaped* up from behind the cow—
A ghostie! Or he *seemed* to be:
with his slight stance
and his wild ruckish crown of pale hair.

We stared a moment at each other
'till he grinned, and held up his pail:
"Less than half a bloody bucket!"

I ne'er spoke a word, but watched him
gather his other empty pail
and weave his way unsteadily
through that very unkept trail;
bits of warm milk
sploshing out on one side…

And as I watched him disappear
back into the woods, I wondered
What kind of bloody farmer hoped
to milk a cow at midnight?

*Ah, well…*I thought to myself,
that'd be the same bloody kind
hoping to chat one up
Christmas Eve…

—Vox clamantis in deserto
"a voice crying out in the wilderness"
(The Motto of Dartmouth College)

clearing out the irises

They cleared out the old Rayzor homestead in Denton,
seemed to pluck it right out of the earth,
leaving a ring of old lonely looking oak trees.

How sad, I thought at first.
How sad that something
so old and beautiful
could just be dug up and carted away,
and the land sectioned and sold.

So I slipped onto the property one day
before the bulldozers arrived,
and made my way across the acreage
and into the hole
where the old house used to be,
my skirt, soaking in dirt
that hadn't seen the sun for at least 100 years,
and felt a *heartbeat* in the soil.

And I recalled walking with my grandmother,
our fists full of trowels
and big brown grocery sacks,
making our way
out to the massive clump of irises
growing thick beneath the oak trees
by her house.
We'd stop and admire all those luscious blooms
of purple and yellow and pink and white,
and then get to work,
digging out spaces in between them.
I'd put my hand in that cool, damp earth—
so ripe with possibilities—
and wonder what beauties would sprout up next...

(continues)

That is the nature of things, I suppose...
Sometimes, no matter how grand or beautiful,
some of the old
must be dug up and cleared out and carted off
to make space—good growing space—
for all those future glories
that are yet to come.

THE new HaRDSCRaBBLE

A hundred years ago, settlers to Red
River had to cut and tie trees on the
backs of their cars to slow down the violent,

downward acceleration into the valley.
With no electricity, no hot, running water,
it was a tough existence. I talk about

harsh winters, when only *once* have I
been without power; only *once* having
to haul water up from the creek; battling

the elements just to drive, or snow-ski,
or carry firewood (already cut and stacked)
from the barn…yet…you're not here.

You stay away, doing the job you think
you should do, no longer re-aligning
planets for a long weekend away.

These days, I run the kids around town;
do late-night dishes; shovel snow; secure
the gates; catch the rodents; pour my own

drinks; chase off my own nightmares…
Indeed, *these* are the dangerous times,
when your woman learns to lock every

door; learns to build her own fires, and stoke
the flames; learns how many layers of clothes
it takes to keep herself warm in the night.

Dead Coyote Detour

We're all afflicted by Point A to Point B.
Set the alarm. Get to school. Get to work.
Fight the highways. Fight the parking. Fight the deadlines.
rush rush rush
then again the next day, and the next...
until that long weekend arrives—
and you're back on the highway,
rushing to vacation—rushing to a slower place; a slower pace;
cursing the time; cursing the cars.

When, suddenly,
something happens outside the city limits—
the rush gives way to a dead coyote on the side of the road,
and you think about that poor creature,
and your eyes leave the highway
to see the open field, from where he came.
And you look the other way, across the four lanes of certain death,
to see where he must have been going,
and catch a hawk just lifting up into the sky...

Oh, to slow! to stop! to circle! to linger!

So, you take the next exit into the tiny town,
and stop on the Square,
and walk around brick buildings
built before your parents were born—
before your grandparents were born;
before the superhighways;
back when Nature had Her own pathways into town.

This is where the *real* Texas lives—
along redbird-flooded back roads;
lingering on the front porches and pink granite courthouses
along tree-named streets;
the spirits of the old
forever circling;
forever leaping fences and concrete barriers
to find their way back home.

WHY GOD needs a SHOTGUN
(and a few NO TRESPASSING signs)

Digging post holes
is hard labour for a man—
especially in that
irresistible country
between Dumas and Amarillo.
The dirt is pink and dry
and hard. And you sweat
and curse, and your
pectoral muscles scream
after digging just *one* hole—
dreading the next hundred
acres worth.
Plus, all the while, you've
got to be on the lookout
for thorny cactus and
hidden dens of baby rattlers,
knowing momma's just waiting
under that next rock.

Now women have their own
kind of labour, and it's reportedly
painful because Eve just couldn't
keep her hands off God's property.
And men...well...men deserve
their hard labour too, I suppose.
After all, they should *know* better
than to be putting up fences
in God's country to begin with.

I guess some trespasses
just aren't the forgiving kind.

IF ONLY THE ICEMAN COULD HAVE LEARNED TO DRIVE

I never initial the back of my driver's license—
that little box that says it's okay
to donate my body to science when I die.
No, no. Fate and I have a very odd relationship,
and to mark my initials
would give Her my permission to end my life—
skewer my destiny
to where my contribution to humanity
would be greater when I'm dead,
instead of when I'm alive…

Oh no, just look at Ötzi, the Iceman.
Modern day CT scans and forensic study
have revealed that the Iceman was murdered,
an artery piercing arrow was found lodged in his back,
the identifying shaft removed,
his precious copper axe
still laying beside him where he fell.
He and his things were then quickly buried
by the perfect combination of snow and ice
which preserved him for 5,000 years…for today…
for science…so we can learn about
the kind of life man lived in the Stone Age.

Science and the education of modern man
seems so obviously…so *sadly*…Iceman's destiny,
leaving us only to wonder at the destiny
of all those other lives cut so short…

Did he have a wife? Did he father any children?
Is there no one left with the DNA to say a prayer
over his well-preserved, mummified corpse?

(continues)

The next time I'm in Italy, along the Austrian border,
I shall find the most beautiful flowers I can
and cast them down into the Ötztal Alps,
and wonder whose fatted calf
accidentally wandered on to his property;
or which elder's hand
Iceman failed to shake;
or, even *worse*,
which stone still bares his engraved initials—
the initials he unknowingly marked with his axe
the night before, when he was preparing the wheat
and cleaning the red deer for supper.

-after reading "Last Hours of the Iceman" by Stephan S. Hall
in the July 2007 edition of *National Geographic*

CALICHE DUST

Caliche dust
upon the trucks.
August funeral.
West Texas.
Outside.
A family plot atop the drop
of San Angelo's great divide.

Loose bones.
Mesquite.
Cattle haulers.
Heat.
50 Stetsons, pale and straw.
The *only* adornments to be found:
nicknames
and belt buckles
on jeans
(extra tall).

Four state troopers to keep the peace.
Counts are rowdy. "Always are, always been."
Big hands, big hearts, big buxom smiles...
Big mischievous men.

Old stories overflow, for life in Robert Lee
is as simple as a yellow kitchen table.
But pain runs as deep as the blood that seeped
down the stairs from the twins, like Cain and Abel.

(continues)

And there have been:
dead sheep in trees,
brothers lost overseas,
Beloved horses, they've had to kill.
But tribulations make them stronger...
seems to make them just live *longer*,
and solder the iron of their will.

But that which abounds in this torrid Texas town,
isn't just rocks, shotguns and wanderlust,
it's *love* that never ends: for Johnny Cash, for kin, for friends—
love as constant as the dry caliche dust.

- attending a Counts family funeral in the town of Robert Lee, Texas

Retirement: NO Maydays

It seemed fitting enough, to hold his retirement party there,
in that old airline building.
A 1958 American Airlines plane sat in silver splendor
in the middle of the room, its head, facing upwards,
towards those high, spotless windows;
forever gazing into that endless sky
it had so easily climbed on a daily basis.

I couldn't help but wonder what that plane must think now,
propped up and quiet, in its polished, immobile state...
how it must long for the feel of the wind;
the El Paso mudrains; the salt of Galveston;
those wicked Pampa ice storms...

The man retiring didn't speak much either,
just a few thank yous to the crowd;
but I saw him stare out the window,
when he thought no one was looking,
his silver hair in full flight
where his brown locks once held strong...

And my husband, next to me, had that same look—
stealing his own glimpses out the window,
perspiration beaded up on his forehead,
his hands tugged at his flat blue tie.

It was then I realized, *this* was his idea of hell—
of standing still; declaring an end;
knowing that from now on, he'll only be able
to *look* at the endless greatness
he once so effortlessly conquered,
while trapped inside
a woman's polished windowed world
of punch and cookies and nice conversation...

(continues)

And, in that moment…I let him go.
No more talk about retirement plans;
or late nights at the office;
or smoking, or drinking, or diet…
because I realized, what he wanted most in this life,
was to fall, flaming from the sky,
in full engine malfunction;
or out of gas; or shot down—

suddenly silenced on the conference call airways;
slumped over his big desk calendar;
a slight grin
filling up Wednesday's little square—
cancelling out
his next three o'clock appointment.

LIVING CLOSE TO DFW AIRPORT,
SEPTEMBER 12, 2001

How often I complained
about airplane traffic;
about the constant noise;
the cluttered horizon;
the disfigured constellations.

And how I cried, that September 12th,
standing in the driveway, face pressed
to the sky—listening, *searching...*
finding nothing but the drop-jaw shock
of Orion.

STRANDED

Strangely, it's more comforting
to find cattle grouped together
in a feed lot; or loaded up for

the meat-market, than to see one,
stranded or lost. Domestic creatures,
they've come to rely on the hand of man—

the spinning windmill; the hay-dropping
truck—becoming nervous; *afraid* to be
away from the herd...And driving north,

on Highway 45, somewhere between
Normangee and Rice, just after the
surge of Hurricane Rita, I came across

a cow, up to her chest in a flooded field.
Stuck, I feared, since she lacked that
heavy-headed gait...I think of her often,

wondering if her desperate brawl ever
reached her rancher's ears, or if it just bounced,
unanswered, from her wide, frightened eyes;

off the river's rising waters; and back,
off the tightly-rolled windows
of each northbound, speeding truck.

persistence

I followed the plains; followed the plains;
past the cotton; past the grain;
past the flat; past gold
hawks…And past
old

Amarillo, off a road—poured and
pocked, the plains dropped in a great
canyon! I gaped, stunned.
Two doves flew
out

of my eyes; doves, *our* birds, flew out of
my eyes; down; down, skimming rough,
Palo Duro rims;
down; down, past
pinked,

millennium scars; down; down, to the
yawning river below—to
cool….to drink…then fly
back up; back
in

to my eyes; these birds, *love* birds; to make
love in my head; beaks, thin beaks,
still wet with drink from
a river
so

slight, birds ruffled and bathed; a river
so slight, that it soaked, dried and
stayed on the bellies
of doves—right
there,

(continues)

inside my head. Look what can happen
when you follow the plains; look
what can happen when
you veer off
man's

roads; when you unleash your eyes—a wisp
of air stirred by wing, flute and
wind; a taste of pink
persistent
time,

sculpting; sculpting canyons without end.

Fry Street Saints

Every*one* and every *place* has their saints.
Italian sailors have San Nicola. Travelers
have St. Christopher. Lovers have St. Valentine;
my Spanish neighbours, their Saint Lupe.

But up here, we're a little different...
here, we're a bit *North of Ordinary*.
Give us the streets; the universities;
the oxygen bars; the piercing parlours.

Here, where housewives are poets
laureate; where kids trade in their cars
for bari-saxes named *Lola*; where the
local superhero wears orange; where

the school of Jupiter boasts more
PhD's per square foot than any ivy
league; where life and faith and art
are inextricably fused together, *our*

saints sit, watchful, in a cement diner,
rethroned to a building of energy and
power...*We* are the church of the living;
consider halos a bit too passé...see

how we toss them aside, in saintly fashion,
preferring our bare heads covered in
gimme caps, or newsboys; or Stetsons;
or mounds of perfectly coiffed platinum...

—written for the unveiling of the saved Fry Street Mural
       in Denton, Texas on April 3o, 2oo9.
          A cinderblock mural, it was an icon of Fry Street,
          and when the building was demolished, it was saved
          and restored and mounted to the outside of the Center
          for Visual Arts (which is an old power plant.) The mural
          features The Beaver, The Beatles, John Wayne, and
          Marilyn Monroe in a diner.

woman in the pipe shop

Amid the intoxicating scents
of man, and leather,
and sweetened burley,
and latakia,
she kissed him—
a deep lover's inhalation
of lips and breath and tongue—
not realizing every pipe stilled;
every struck match, burned;
every conversation, paused...
all dazed in the discovery
of the perfect, unnamed blend
of earth and flesh and fire.

COMING OF AGE

I was always amazed how people can get up
when they don't have to,
when there's no place they have to be;
no time clock checking their tardiness.

I see them as I'm rushing out in the morning—
a victim of not enough hours for work,
not enough sleep.
Yet they are there, completely awake; completely aware;
I used to think it was just an age thing,
but maybe, in a way, it is…

Maybe we reach a point in our lives
when we can actually catch up to our needs—
begin to *live* instead of just survive.

Maybe we reach a time like in '07, when the long Texas drought
that plagued farmers for decades, was officially declared over—
when the rains had finally caught up to the hungry, thirsting earth.

A time when farmers could turn their attentions
away from the shriveling roots and cracked soil,
and lift their eyes a bit higher—
to marvel at the variegated greens of the leaves,
and lean their heads into the white blooming limbs
for a long, deep, thankful smell
of all things fruitful and beautiful and alive.

PICKING UP THE ACCENT

My husband calls me a chameleon,
says that everywhere I go,
I pick up the accent,
sounding just like a local
within a few months of living there.
I had no idea I did that.

I wonder if it's the food...

But maybe that's what
finding your own voice
is all about.
Maybe it's not so much
about where we're from,
but where we've *been*
that matters.

We ingest every experience.

All those heartbreaks and sunsets
and music and kisses
seep into the bone,
curve the hand around the pen,
streak the hair, deepen the dimples,
and lilt the vocabulary
like quick whiskey to the tongue...
We can't help but bring it *all* to the table.

It took me 2 hours and 42 years to write this poem.

(continues)

Perhaps one day, I'll travel to the moon
and learn the accent of silence
from the barren craters and powdered Tang,
and mix it all in
with the Florida sunshine and citrus;
the Carolina society and sugar;
the New Orleans *'Laissez les bon temps rouler'*
and gumbo;
the cowboy boots and Tex-Mex;
(and all those other places I've yet to know)
and *then* see what voice emerges
the next time I come to the table
and sit down to write a poem.

acknowledgments

a.k.a. Elvis, Zone Press

Alamo Coastline, Zone Press

After, *Write Around the Corner*

Bad Theology, *Illya's Honey*

Becoming Superman, *Ardent*, Zone Press

Bursting Into Snowflakes, *Ardent*

Caliche Dust, *Langdon Review*

Charm Bracelet, Zone Press

Christmas at Love Field, *Oak Bend Review*

Dead Coyote Detour, *Ardent*

Death and Soapboxes, Aisle 5, *Langdon Review*

Don't Be Nervous, *Write Around the Corner*, Zone Press

For Love and Michelangelo, *Concho River Review*

Graveside in Sanger, *New Texas*

Hanging On, *Amarillo Bay*

Horse Latitudes, *Langdon Review*, Zone Press

Inside Fat Quarters, *Redefining Beauty*, Dos Gatos Press

Picking up the Accent, Zone Press

Pictographs, *Ardent*

San Nicola Intercessions, *Oak Bend Review*

Searching for Ascension, *Texas Poetry Calendar*, (Dos Gatos Press)

Shattering the Ordinary, Zone Press

Smoke Rings over Wichita County, *Langdon Review*

Superman's Birthday, *descant*

The Closer, Zone Press

The Real Story of How Quanah Parker Brought the Wisdom of Jesus Christ to the Native Americans, *Langdon Review*

Tumbleweed Philosophy, *Langdon Review*

What Clings to the Back of the Spoon, Zone Press

When Texas No Longer Fits In the Glove Box, Texas Poetry Calendar, *Big Land; Big Sky; Big Hair Anthology* (both by Dos Gatos Press)

Where Moonlight Cannot Tread, *Denton Writer's League Anthology*

Wildfire DNA, *Langdon Review*

Woman in the Pipe Shop, *Southwestern American Literature*

ABOUT THE AUTHOR

Karla K. Morton, a Fort Worth native, now of Denton, has had her
work published in esteemed literary journals, electronic and in print.
Morton's work has appeared in such publications as *Amarillo Bay*,
REAL, *descant*, *Langdon Review*, *New Texas*, *Illya's Honey*, *Borderlands*,
and *Southwestern American Literature*.

    Wee Cowrin' Timorous Beastie, her book/ CD released by
Lagniappe in 2007, blends poetry and original music by the Canadian
composer, Howard Baer. The poet followed *Wee Cowrin' Timorous
Beastie* with *Redefining Beauty*, a book of poetry and photographs,
published by Dos Gatos Press in 2009. In *Redefining Beauty*, Morton
writes from experience about her will to survive breast cancer.

    In 2010 Morton has three other new releases: *Becoming
Superman* (Zone Press); *Stirring Goldfish* (Finishing Line Press); and
Names We've Never Known (the Texas Review Press) in addition to the
TCU Press title.

karla k. morton
new and selected poems

ISBN 978-0-87565-414-0

Case. $15.95

TCU Texas Poets Laureate Series

ISBN 978-0-87565-414-0

9 780875 654140

51595